Legendary Bigfoot

Candice Ransom

Lerner Publications ◆ Minneapolis

Lerner Publications Company
An imprint of Lerner Publishing Group, Inc.
241 First Avenue North
Minneapolis, MN 55401 USA

For reading levels and more information, look up this title at www.lernerbooks.com.

Main body text set in Billy Infant regular.
Typeface provided by SparkType.

Editor: Alison Lorenz

Library of Congress Cataloging-in-Publication Data

Names: Ransom, Candice F., 1952- author.
Title: Legendary bigfoot / Candice Ransom.
Description: Minneapolis : Lerner Publications, 2021. | Series: Lightning bolt books—spooked! | Includes bibliographical references and index. | Audience: Ages 6-9 | Audience: Grades 2-3 | Summary: "For decades, people have spotted a tall, hairy creature in the woods of the Pacific Northwest. But is Bigfoot truly real, or just a silly prank? Discover the truth about Bigfoot in this creepy tale" —Provided by publisher.
Identifiers: LCCN 2019040491 (print) | LCCN 2019040492 (ebook) | ISBN 9781541596900 (library binding) | ISBN 9781728400495 (ebook)
Subjects: LCSH: Sasquatch—Juvenile literature.
Classification: LCC QL89.2.S2 R36 2020 (print) | LCC QL89.2.S2 (ebook) | DDC 001.944—dc23

LC record available at https://lccn.loc.gov/2019040491
LC ebook record available at https://lccn.loc.gov/2019040492

Manufactured in the United States of America
1-47796-48236-12/3/2019

Table of Contents

What Is Bigfoot?

A hiker is lost in a dark forest. Huge pine trees hide the sun. Suddenly the hiker sees a giant shape between the trees.

A tall, hairy creature comes closer. The beast stares at the hiker. Then it turns and disappears into the woods. The hiker believes he has seen Bigfoot.

People have told stories about Bigfoot for many years. They say the monster looks like an ape. But it walks on legs like a human and leaves very large footprints.

People see Bigfoot in North America. Sightings happen mostly in the woods of California, Oregon, and Washington. Some have seen Bigfoot in Canada.

Many people like to visit places where Bigfoot has been seen.

Bigfoot Everywhere

Creatures similar to Bigfoot appear around the world. Stories say Yeti climbs the snowy mountains of Tibet. In Australia, people claim half-man, half-ape Yowie hides in the hills.

American Indian stories include a hairy beast called Sasquatch. It has long arms, big feet, and lives in the forests of the American West.

In 1958, a California road worker named Jerry Crew found mysterious tracks. He made a plaster cast of a huge footprint to take to the local newspaper.

The footprints Crew found looked like those of a very large man.

Crew told the newspaper editor a strange beast was in the area. The footprint was proof. The newspaper published the story. **They named the creature Bigfoot.**

After the first newspaper story, other papers and news shows talked about Bigfoot too.

Chasing Bigfoot

The newspaper story made people curious about Bigfoot. In 1967, two men went to find Bigfoot in Northern California. One man brought a movie camera.

In the woods, they saw a tall, furry creature by a stream. The man filmed the animal hurrying away. It looked back at them and then disappeared.

This picture comes from the men's 1967 film of the strange animal.

From far away, a man in a gorilla suit could look like Bigfoot.

The men showed the film to scientists. Some said it was a man in a gorilla suit. Others said the creature was real. Years later, scientists continue to study the film.

Many people have searched for Bigfoot. Others meet to talk about the creature. Hunting Bigfoot is popular in movies and TV shows. **But is Bigfoot real?**

Groups such as Sasquatch Watch organize to look for Bigfoot.

Finding Bigfoot

The mysterious tracks Crew found in 1958 were fake. Another worker made the tracks as a joke. But no one knew until 2002.

In 1976, a man claimed he saw Bigfoot between two trees. He pulled hair off some tree bark. He sent the hair to the FBI to test. The FBI report said the hair was from a deer.

Some scientists say that if Bigfoot were real, people would have captured it long ago. Blurry photos and movies claim to show Bigfoot. But we have no true proof that Bigfoot is real.

People jokingly put up signs around places with many Bigfoot sightings.

Many people want to find Bigfoot. They believe the big, hairy creature of legend is out there.

Close Encounter

Robert Hatfield's dogs would not stop barking. He went outside and saw a hairy, manlike creature. It must be Bigfoot! The beast knocked him down. He hurried into the house with the creature on his heels. It tried to break down his door! Suddenly, the beast left. Would anyone believe Hatfield's story? Afterward, he found a huge, muddy handprint on the side of the house.

Terrifying Trivia

- People say Bigfoot has a strong, unpleasant odor. It doesn't smell like any other animal.
- Washington State has had the most Bigfoot sightings. People have also seen Bigfoot in California, Pennsylvania, Michigan, New York, Ohio, Oregon, and Texas.
- Those who have seen Bigfoot say it is about 6 to 10 feet (1.8 to 3 m) tall. They described its hair as black, brown, red brown, gray, or white.

Glossary

ape: an animal such as a chimpanzee or gorilla

curious: eager to learn about

fake: not real

FBI: short for Federal Bureau of Investigation, a part of the government that investigates crimes

legend: a story told often over a long time

plaster: a paste made of water and sand that hardens when it dries

sighting: when someone claims to see something

Further Reading

Bigfoot Facts for Kids
https://kids.kiddle.co/Bigfoot

Jones, Molly. *Bigfoot.* New York: AV2 by Weigl, 2020.

Kallio, Jamie. *Investigating Sasquatch*. New York: AV2 by Weigl, 2019.

Ransom, Candice. *Mysterious Loch Ness Monster.* Minneapolis: Lerner Publications, 2021.

"Sasquatch—Our Furry Friends?"
https://www.cbc.ca/kidscbc2/the-feed/sasquatch-our-furry-friends

Index

Photo Acknowledgments

Image credits: RichLegg/Getty Images, pp. 2, 5, 23; Kichigin/Shutterstock.com, p. 4; aleks1949/Getty Images, p. 6; JudeAnd/Shutterstock.com, p. 7; Daniel Eskridge/istock/Getty Images, p. 8; RichVintage/Getty Images, p. 9; C and L Perry/Shutterstock.com, p. 10; tomazl/Getty Images, p. 11; Adrian Green/Getty Images, p. 12; Bettmann/Getty Images, p. 13; 4x6/Getty Images, p. 14; The Washington Post/Getty Images, p. 15; Igor Shoshin/Shutterstock.com, p. 16; awhelin/iStock/Getty Images, p. 17; Teri Virbickis/Shutterstock.com, p. 18; Jonhy Blaze/Getty Images, p. 19.

Cover images: THEPALMER/Getty Images; RikoBest/Shutterstock.com.